EXIT ORPHEUS

Library of Congress Cataloging-in-Publication Data
Hong, Matthew.
Exit Orpheus / Matthew Hong.
LCCN: 2009902641

ISBN 978-0-9791184-2-5

Published by Aria Press, New York
www.exitorpheus.com

Matthew Hong

AVANT PROPOS

It would not be without reluctance and perhaps too, some remorse, that I should publish this piece.

This work would be conceived towards the latter months of the final redaction of the epic poem, *I, Faust.* The succession of one forgotten form after another would seem twice-fold futile. Adding to this, yet another impossible legend, Orpheus. And as customary, it could not be a homage to the beauty of his vertiginous song, but rather his final shrill and tragic gesture still resounding in the halls of Hades.

I would often wonder about the chosen trajectory of my artistic formation and my feeling obliged to move in these terms. I had for some time certain verses strident in the veins, circulating an unsettling kind of homeostasis, pulsating for another insufferable task–the phantom pains in the aftermath of a twenty-year project finally let go. –Or more decidedly, the inert resin of everything unaccomplished of an otherwise unfortunate life.

Many times I had tried to evacuate these lines which had formed but lingered unarticulated. The published abstract of *Cities & Dust* was to be something of a chronicling, however without much condolence in its epistolary respiration.

So I would descend into my purgatory and resurface with this thing all too personal and without levity. Granted, this work would be much less autobiographical in scope than any previous attempt, but was to bear a deliberate resemblance to a reality which I was to just barely survive and from which I would wander forever marked.

I would since uproot myself to foreign territories, acclimate to a different tongue, no doubt with a drive to distance myself from the refuse of all this, to forget the English language as it were, and to deny its poetry which for me had been for a major period a kind of life force.

Though I may be no less compromising at present, I could say without any affectation that my general disposition was much more serious before when I was twenty than today as I approach forty. I was stronger then than I am now. I would think of those who preceded me and wonder whether I had not over-dwelled in this domain. I had been feeling the progressive decline of my life as a writer. There would eventually be an argument woven for my having restrained myself in my first pursuit of painting and the fine arts–anything from embarking on this path where inspiration was to be long since struck from the manifest

and whatever aspiration wrested away and waylaid.
Perhaps I had been summoned to assume the fallow
strains of my own dissolution. I had effectively written
myself into an improbable abyss, with such a terrible
finale in the treatment of Faust, I was to believe I would
never again rise after. One does not simply scribe an
epic poem, one survives it. The only explanation for my
continuing is brut insanity, or the absurd adherence to that
forsaken presumption that I should somehow faithfully
remain a poet.

Now having written it, I am unable to place this work
in the greater scope of things. This piece would once be
described as Shakespeare meeting Mamet, dining with
Robbe-Grillet. Somewhat germanic in treatment and
undeniably post-structuralist, it would be quite concise
in its purpose, at parts even terse. —Understood, very little
to illuminate its reason for being. Why I should concede
to release this would remain concealed. Having derived no
comfort in its dialectical opposite would have its perennial
Socratic persuasion. Perhaps I had found pretext with
the premise that it was a theater piece and thus open to
adaptation, perhaps a sense of comfort that its readership
or audience in any event was destined to be quite limited.
I might be excused given my near conviction that this
would be the last thing I should ever put to page. I would
thus provoke the extradition of these words to their
appointed vessel. Admittedly, there had been a desire to
bury this thing entirely, or continue working on it for
the next twenty years, which would undoubtedly amount
to the same.

Surely the errors of judgment in the life of a man abound.
Whereas, I had not been absolved of such tendencies in
any of the aspects of my own existence, nor discharged

from the various pursuits making up such patterns which presupposed for me a semblance of some meaning.

Whereas, in the face of this reality there is a will to abstain from any engagement of action, or at least to not make any sudden motions. With age I would move more and more in default rather than in defiance.

Whereas, I should not be consoled, nor my faith restituted, in the reception of this work, as had been clearly the case with the previous work. My naivete, unlike my vanity, would have its apparent and proper limits. And my pride would have long since been abashed.

Therefore, with distinct humility, and with whatever reverence might be preserved in me, I would dedicate this piece to the *one,* to whom I had been unable to dedicate, among other things, my previous work.

I would present this here, now while I should still be capable, before my words truly resound as those of a dead man. And so it would come to pass, my own backward gaze, impertinent and so full of noise, and still poised for pardon.

– M.H. / 2008

There is still a great pain
in my heart.

There is still that vast emptiness
within me.

I have tore at my insides with
words as knives,

And nothing came of it.

I have become entirely inelegant
and strange.

–from Epitaph

DRAMATIS PERSONAE:

MAN
WOMAN

MISE EN SCENE:

Center stage, two Barcelona chairs facing slightly
outward; A coffee table in between with a cell phone
and a magazine; A kitchen island counter centered
in the back; Camera equipment and lights clustered
next to it; A window suspended to the left, mid-
stage, a mirror to the right; A simple black stool in
the front, to the side; Otherwise, everything black.

SCENE I

[*MAN is looking out the window.*
WOMAN is obscured in the background.]

MAN: Once again I contend with
the dissipation of
          moonlight and
the slight notion that I have lost my way.
What shall we say
          of this erosion
of time, imperceptible and
contiguous yet
          partitioned
and made incremental by our own
construct? This
          course beyond
instruction, a force unyielding,
inscrutable. Strident
          like the sound
I make when I make a sound.
Inertia and kinetics
          of descent.

[*WOMAN emerges.*]

WOMAN: There is no looking back on those
things. Wayward
          without resolve.
There is no otherwise for those years,
Those lives involved,
          this life.

MAN: I gaze over the rooftops reflecting

the night sky
              like surfaces
of lakes frozen in winter.

WOMAN: It is not yet winter.

[*MAN, without moving his body, slowly
turns his head towards WOMAN. Pause. . . .
Lights flicker with a buzzing sound.*]

MAN: It seems not possible to know
the desires of others,
                    only wanting.

WOMAN: There is nothing more to know.

[*WOMAN turns away. She collects herself,
and makes a motion to brush off lint
from her dress.*]

It was good of you to come.

[*MAN begins to set up the tripod, the
lights, and the portrait style camera near
the back. WOMAN prepares herself,
half propped on the stool. After some
movement, a moment of stillness.*]

–Though, I was expecting you last night.

[*Pause.*]

MAN: I was indisposed. And anyway,
I was not prepared
                    to see you.

WOMAN: You could have called.

> [*MAN fires a test of the strobes, takes
> a light reading, loads a cartridge.*]

MAN: I sent you a text message.

WOMAN: Strange, I didn't receive anything.

> [*MAN winds the camera, presses the
> cable shutter release. Strobes flash on.
> He pulls paper. Pulls film. He places the
> shot on the kitchen counter. The captured
> image is projected on the back wall for
> a moment, then dissolves into black.*]

You could have called.

MAN: I still don't understand why you
wouldn't prefer
a real photographer.

WOMAN: I need these test shots by tomorrow.
I wanted you
to take them.

> [*Wind. Click / flash. Pull paper. Pull film.*]

How have you been?

MAN: —Not well, I'm afraid.

> [*Wind. Click / flash. Pull paper. Pull film.*]

WOMAN: You never did come back
for your things.

MAN: I am here now.

[*Wind. Click / flash. Pull paper. Pull film.*]

WOMAN: Will you be leaving in the morning?

MAN: I shall be leaving tonight.

[*Wind. Click / flash. Pull paper. Pull film.*]

WOMAN: You still wear the ring.

[*MAN glances at his hand.*]

MAN: You still haven't told me what
these photos are for.

WOMAN: They are for the concert program.

[*Wind. Click / flash. Pull paper. Pull film.*]

MAN: I wasn't aware you started
performing again.

[*Pause.*]

WOMAN: It's just a recital at the conservatory.
I haven't yet
decided whether or not
I will submit these photos.

[*WOMAN looks away. Pause.*]

Perhaps you will think this whole
evening a pretext.

MAN: It doesn't matter what I think.

[*Wind. Click / flash. Pull paper. Pull film.*]

WOMAN: I will be performing your pieces.

MAN: –And turn.

[*WOMAN turns slightly as lights increase.
Wind. Click / flash. Pull paper. Pull film.*]

–A bit more.

[*WOMAN turns more, slightly agitated.
Wind. Click / flash. Pull paper. Pull film.*]

–Now profile.

[*WOMAN showing profile to the camera.
Wind. Click / flash. Pull paper. Pull film.
Short pause. MAN steps in front of the
camera, stares intently at her. WOMAN,
still showing profile, looks down, aware of
his gaze. Pause for an extended moment
during which the lights gradually go up,
overly bright, then back down to normal.*]

Your beauty still astounds me.

[*WOMAN rises from the stool and moves
to one of the chairs, takes a seat.*]

WOMAN: You only think that when you
photograph me.

MAN: I see you in a different light.

WOMAN: You capture me as an object.

MAN: I capture you in your essence.
—But not in these photos.

[*Lights dim.*]

.

SCENE II

[*WOMAN is looking out the window,
MAN is facing the mirror.*]

WOMAN: After all this time without speaking
I admit I was
                    uncertain whether
you would come.

MAN: I said I would be here. I am here.

WOMAN: I am sorry to learn you are not well.
I should perhaps
                    offer you a drink.

MAN: —Yes. That would be lovely.

[*WOMAN goes behind the kitchen
counter and fixes two drinks. She takes
a moment to look at the photos. MAN
paces about, moves to the window.*]

I have taken that promenade.
I have observed
                    the horizon at dusk
and found myself trapped
against the lines
                    which faded into
the slate-colored sky. I have
driven out of town
                    only to turn
around late and return before

arriving anywhere.
                    I have stood
in the midnight rain under
dizzying lights
                    by the street corners
stark of any occurrence, obscured
by the darkness.
                    I have composed
stupid ballads. I have slept
through my days.
                    I have waited
motionless in my room. I have
wept. And I
                    made no sound.

WOMAN: I am sorry to hear you are not well.

[*WOMAN hands him a drink and takes a
seat. MAN sits opposite her, looks around
the room as if just arrived for the first
time. He slowly rattles the ice in his glass.*]

MAN: I have become tired of the city.
The menacing traffic,
                    the constant
chorus of irreverent honking,
the callousness
                    of cab drivers. . . .
I saw today on the sidewalk,
an insolent child
                    with his mother
—the mother then disembodied
of any motherhood—
                    and the bigoted

bystander watching in disbelief.
–That would be me.
                              And then again,
the cab drivers. . . . And so on
into the offices
                    of power-hungry
politicians, bullying businessmen,
and the conceit
                    of corporations.

WOMAN: *You* are a corporation.

[*WOMAN rises, looks out the window.
MAN crosses his arms, grasps his throat.*]

Spring and summer passed. Passing.
A life lived.
                    Living. Nearly
four decades of movement and
stillness alternating
                        and confounded.
And you have only tried to hold on
to the twilight
                    breeze. And I,
I have lived a life of strained sorrow.
With carelessness
                    borrowed
I have faulted and I have paid
dearly. And I am
                    still paying. . . .
This cannot be the end. Yet
there seems little
                    left to say.

MAN: Winter will not warm us.

WOMAN: Probably.

[*MAN rises, looks into the mirror.*]

MAN: I have seen death. Its face
like a woman,
             I have tried to wed.

WOMAN: Woman as death–a bit morbid, no?
What sort of woman?

MAN: . . . To return to that old oblivion
from a life left
          of desire.

WOMAN: –Released of the object. To desire
nothing is death.

MAN: Yes, less morbid.

[*MAN moves over to look at the photos.*]

I have thought of you. I have missed
seeing you
          sipping your porto.
That look of surprise, always
after the first try.
              Even with
the glass empty, the way
you would bring it
            to your lips . . .
And in your solemn sadness,
how I wanted
         to reach out.

I had a vision of you, sitting
on a bench.
            Your eyes glazed
as if with tears, wanting to
say something.
            You had
one leg swinging, like a child,
your finger
            playing with
the button of your jacket.

WOMAN: That was not me. You confuse
me with another.

MAN: . . . And how it never took much
to make you happy.

WOMAN: Yet, you would later withhold
those favors.

MAN: Strange. I still look for you
in the crowd,
            hoping to get
a glimpse. I sometimes revisit
those places
            where we were,
where you might be again. I have
felt myself a stalker.

WOMAN: You need only call me.

[*Pause. MAN moves back towards
the window.*]

MAN: Things have caught up with me.
It is true, I had
                wanted to see you
but I could not reason my wanting
against the backdrop
                of my newly
found disposition, being as I am–

WOMAN: What ill disposition might that be?

[*MAN sits down, starts to rub his face
with both hands.*]

MAN: The delicacy of my present
sensibilities,
            the anxiety I suffer
as a modality, the frailty it seems
of my entire being
            –everything,
such that the slightest sound
is enough to
           thrust me into this
state of complete derangement.
I have not worked
           on anything since
my departure last fall, adding to it
the month of August
           also idle. I had
tried writing new material. And
its consequence:
           Boredom, effeteness.

[*The phone rings–in a loud, hyper-modern
ring tone.*]

–That's rather annoying.

[*WOMAN picks up the phone, looks at it.
She does not answer but stops the ringing.*]

WOMAN: You're quite irritable.

[*MAN picks up the magazine from the
table, begins to flip through. WOMAN
observes him. Pause with silence.*]

MAN: –Unbelievable.

[*Flipping a few more pages, then pausing.*]

      –Utterly flaccid. . . .
People are publishing silly poems
under fake names
          of famous poets.

WOMAN: I usually just look through the cartoons.

[*MAN puts the magazine down.
He gets up and moves to the window.
Resumes rubbing his face, then stops
to look at his hands.*]

MAN: –I do this now, as if I needed
to confirm that
        my face were
still there. Funny how we age.

[*WOMAN is biting her finger nail.*]

WOMAN: I noticed you picked up a tick or two.

[*The phone rings again.*]

MAN: —That's quite annoying.

[*WOMAN looks at MAN, then answers the phone.*]

WOMAN: *Pronto?*

[*WOMAN rises and paces to the back to speak privately. MAN pulls out his own phone from his jacket and begins to press a few buttons, then uses two hands as if typing a message. He stops after a moment when he sees she is nearly done. WOMAN reemerges.*]

MAN: Who was it?

WOMAN: —No one important.

MAN: Yes, of course.

[*Extended pause while they pace around.*]

WOMAN: What remains now but memories?
Shared photos.
              Old letters.
Such small things. We would do well
to destroy them.
              Our past ritual of
exchanging affection, which could not
amount to much
              then, will now form

the outline of a dream recounted.

MAN: —But only a dream. A careful
reconstitution of
                    what could have
been with minor variations.

WOMAN: It's been some time since we've exchanged
anything worthwhile
                        or even good.

[*Pause.*]

MAN: My gestures were true, my letters
honest. At least
                at the time
when they were written. Life, love,
and art . . . perhaps
                        I chose wrongly.
Each seemed exclusive of the others.
In my refusal
            to bend in any
of the three, I ended with none.

[*Pause.*]

. . . Thinking we had loved once,
realizing now we
                    had not loved well.
And if it be that I had been shown
beauty, I know
                nothing of it now.

[*Pause.*]

WOMAN: Your cynicism and fatigue like a
virus in your
         blood coursing its
finite path. This cannot be your legacy.

MAN: Legacy or no, I'm afraid there is
little left of me
       otherwise.

[*Lights dim.*]

SCENE III

[*WOMAN is on the chair, sitting stiffly
on the edge, her hands on her knees.
MAN stands behind her, his hands resting
on the back of her chair as if at a podium.*]

WOMAN: I have missed you.

[*MAN walks a few steps around the chair,
looks away. Begins to rub his face.*]

MAN: What happened to us?

[*Pause.*]

WOMAN: You betrayed me.

[*WOMAN gets up, moves to the mirror.*]

MAN: I have not betrayed you, yet.

[*WOMAN turns abruptly to look at
MAN. She lets out a nervous laugh,
then quickly becomes silent.*]

WOMAN: –Could we start again?

[*Pause without movement. Lights dim
half way. WOMAN returns to the chair.
MAN resumes his position behind her
as before. Lights up.*]

I have missed you.

[*Pause.*]

MAN: I have missed you, as well.

[*MAN walks a few steps around the chair.*]

WOMAN: What happened to us?

[*WOMAN gets up and moves to the mirror.*]

MAN: We are, both of us, to blame.

WOMAN: –I blame you.

[*MAN looks over the photos.*]

MAN: Two people meet. Fall in love.
And proceed to
      annihilate each other.

WOMAN: This is your war . . . of which
I want no part.

MAN: I was once a man of peace. You neglect
your half in this
      counterpoint.

[*Pause. MAN looks down at his glass
and starts to rattle the ice again.*]

WOMAN: That's annoying.

[*Pause. He puts his glass down on the table.*]

MAN: You were always the auditor

of my undocumented
                    emotions.
You policed my best intentions.
You arrested me
                on my affectations.

[*Pause. He grasps at his throat.*]

–I'm sorry, this is not working. . . .

[*Lights dim half way. WOMAN returns
to the chair. This time she is reclined, shoes
off, legs crossed, one foot touching the floor,
the other on the seat, one arm over the
back of the seat. MAN resumes his position
behind the chair as before. Lights up.*]

WOMAN: I have missed you.

[*Pause. MAN looks down at WOMAN.
WOMAN looks about. She is unaware of
his stare, but exhibits mild discomfort.*]

MAN: I . . . have missed you, too. I have
missed the scent
                of your sex on my
hands, my lips. And your hungered
mouth awakening
                me into a dream.
The rise and fall of your perfect
breasts when you
                slept, your legs
which spread before me as the
ultimate possibility.
                I shall not

relive these moments, I regret.

[*WOMAN slips on her shoes, rises and looks into the mirror. She begins to put on lipstick. MAN watches her and does not move.*]

WOMAN: By your touch I had been
transformed.
            You entered me
through a kiss. You filled me
with your song.
                 We were good
together. Then day turned into
night and night
                into day. You were
no longer present, and I descended
into darkness.
             Even as you return
you regather yourself for your exit.

MAN: It was not to last. Founded on
innocence and
              desire, sustained by
a diminishing hope, held together
by labor, later let go.
             At last divided
by the growing indifference.

[*WOMAN moves to the window, looks out.*]

WOMAN: In the beginning, it was good.

[*She cracks a smile, then releases it, biting the side of her lower lip. Pause.*]

We made passage
            like foreigners
through unknown continents.
Everything was new.
                        We were in
love. We were all that mattered.
Gypsies without
                  landing. It was
different then. *You* were different.

MAN: It was not easy for you, I recall.

WOMAN: —I didn't mind.

MAN: You often complained.

WOMAN: —I am a woman.

[*Pause. She moves to the mirror.*]

I sometimes wonder, if only we could
meet again, as
                  for the first time. . . .

MAN: It would turn out the same.

WOMAN: Of course. You would end in
reorchestrating this.

MAN: With the help of fate we have
both had our
                  hands in this.
It was not my role alone.

[*Rattling his ice.*]

Perhaps a certain destiny
over which we
                    had no control.

WOMAN: Fate. Destiny. These words
have lost all
                    signification.
You continue to employ them. But
you are better
                    than this. And
you have done nothing to counter
this movement.
                              It served you. And
you would not have had it otherwise.

MAN: The dark angels have compelled
me as such.
                    You alone will prevail
as the true heroine of this drama.

WOMAN: You always were my angel in black.

MAN: –Your death angel.

[*Pause. MAN, a little complacent.*]

In the end, all our wishes proved
to be worthless.
                    You had waited
for me. I might again be waiting
for you. Waiting
                    for the other.

[*Making wide gestures with his glass.*]

I claimed I could stand forever.
You had declared
            you were running
out of time. I had become obstinate.
You had become
            demanding.
We had each of us become tiresome
to the other,
            our words, terse
and no longer of any meaning.

[*MAN goes and pours another drink.*]

How long had I wanted for you to
come to me with
            an open heart,
without the tiredness and the disdain?
I was prepared to
            sacrifice everything.
I *had* sacrificed everything. All I wanted
was for us to be
            fully realized. But
instead, I could but disappoint you.
We were no longer
            innocent. And I
could no longer make you happy.

WOMAN: I never wanted for you to make
those sacrifices.
            I wanted you
to continue your work, your art.

MAN: Wanting me to continue my work
did not help.
            Simply wanting me

to be inspired did not make it so.

WOMAN: Please forgive me.

MAN: How could I forgive you?

[*Pause. WOMAN abruptly returns to her chair mimicking her previously stiff posture.*]

WOMAN: Please forgive me.

MAN: —Yes, of course. I forgive you.

[*Pause. MAN starts to rattle the ice in his glass. WOMAN rises to pace.*]

WOMAN: Why could you not have forgiven me?

MAN: I have forgiven you.

[*WOMAN strikes a look of confusion.*]

WOMAN: Then why must we be apart?
—I don't understand.
                    And why
must we be separated again?

MAN: Not by what you had done,
or what I had
                    done, but because
of who we were and what was to
occur between us
                    henceforth.

WOMAN: That's too complicated.

MAN: Betrayal was pending. It was in
the separation
            that we became
absolved. Because nothing
else mattered.
            There was no other
reason. That was the tragedy.
Perfection imprinted,
            slowly fading.
The music had stopped, silence
prevailed. We were
            not happy.

WOMAN: That does not console me. No.

[*Pause. . . . While lights remain on,
WOMAN slowly returns to her reclined
position on the chair. She looks up
at the lights.*]

What happened to us?

MAN: —I do not know.

[*MAN gradually reclaims his stance
behind the chair.*]

Supposing we had stayed together,
where would we
            be now?

WOMAN: What difference does it make?

MAN: And if I were to return, would you
         then have me?

WOMAN: —Probably not. Not until you
         want me despite
                              everything.

MAN: I want you. —But not despite
         everything. One might
                              prefer it
         because of everything. No?

WOMAN: And anyway, you are too proud
         to come back.
                         You are cruel
         to torment me like this.

MAN: The pain I feel is enough
         for us both.
                         I would not wish it
         upon another.

WOMAN: Still, you would will it upon me.
         It was convenient
                              for you to leave.
         You left. What was I to do?

MAN: Are you quite finished?

WOMAN: —There is more.

MAN: —Yes, to be sure. When I engaged
         you it was not
                              for this. Not for
         the readiness of your quick reply.

WOMAN: You took the easy way out.

MAN: —Nothing is easy.

[*Pause.*]

You indulge in your unaccountability
since our separation.
                          But it was
in accounting everything
we find ourselves
                          at this stage.

WOMAN: You might have thought of other
possibilities.
                          All things are possible;
and only *some* things probable.

[*Lights dim half way. WOMAN returns
to her seat, stiff as before. MAN resumes
his posture behind the chair. Lights up.*]

MAN: What happened to us?

[*Pause. WOMAN tugs at her ear.*]

WOMAN: You had betrayed me.

MAN: I had not betrayed you, then.
In any case, I had
                          not the strength.
I had simply assumed my position.
There is no
                          withdrawing that.

WOMAN: Your indifference was your betrayal.

MAN: You continue to deny your part
in this affair.

WOMAN: You broke my heart.

[*A brief instance uncontrolled.*]

MAN: Yes. . . . Surely the worst thing a man
could do to a woman.
                   Still, you had
broken my will. –The one thing worse
a woman might do
                to a man.

[*Pause.*]

You realize, I still love you.

WOMAN: You cannot console me. There is
no more you
              or I, or anyone,
can do to add, or take away, from
what has already
              come to pass.
You might like to know I had waited
many nights
            in certain vigil. I had
kept my sorrows at bay, in pride.
I had wept, trying
             carefully to
forget you. I could not forget you.
I had dyed my hair,
             erased my smile

that I might become a stranger to myself.
I had bathed in
          cold springs and waited
to be reborn. I had waded through
gardens forlorn to feel
              again a kiss
of fragrant wishes as if of maidens
from the past
          and I passed
undetected. I had at last weighed myself
against the weather
             and found myself
insignificant. I had gazed at the moon
and felt the beast
           inside become afraid
and lost. I had held stray postcards,
its gloss faded
        by my hands,
dreaming to be delivered to a
foreign land,
          if only in my thoughts.
I had danced the macabre dance
with old shadows
          in smoke-filled halls
poised with my *carnet de bal* with your
name on it. I had
          burned this house down
with all the things in it and rebuilt it
only to find the
          chambers and corridors
obscured in the same mystery
and darkness.
         I had cursed the day
we met and there was no effect.

I live now with a knife
                    inside my heart
that twists each time my thoughts start
towards the memory
                    of what used to be.
I had yearned for your return with my
complete being
                    and I despise myself
for it. You cannot console me.
No, you cannot.

[*Lights dim.*]

SCENE IV

[*MAN is looking into the mirror.*
WOMAN is on the chair.]

MAN: Our lives now confounded but
not yet ended.
             Unwoven each day
the same discovery. Unearthing.
I must learn
        again the words.
And also forget. Forgetting.
How we have
        come into being. . . .
Born. Die. Somewhere between,
come alive.
        Live a life.

[*Pause.*]

WOMAN: Look at me. You no longer look
at me. I should
        have known better
than to have involved myself
with you–the *artist.*

MAN: I am no longer to be called an artist.

[*Pause.*]

Having known now excellence in
many minor
        movements, but still
only motions toward nothingness.

Greatness eludes me.
                    I am not yet
arriving, or arrived. I am a man
marked by my own
                    absence.

[*He rattles his ice, looks down at his glass.*]

—There seems a kind of refrain here.
Incapable now,
                    and more and more
difficult the distinction, my world,
my song. So my art
                    has carved me
into this inescapable niche.
In reality and
                    in my thoughts.
I seem no longer in possession
of those faculties.
                    Acquitted now
and released into the void.

WOMAN: Such lament. Such fatigue. You always
        did want to be free
                    of reproach.

[*MAN takes a seat.*]

MAN: And what residue of intelligence
      might I dust
                  from these remains? What
      conquest of knowing claimed from
      this experience?
                  There is not even

the remote calling. Forever now,
made bleak. My
          testament, now reduced
to but a memoir of my madness.

[*The phone rings, this time in a discrete
tone. MAN hesitates, then answers.*]

–*Allô?* . . . Yes . . .

[*Stands.*]

No. . . . Yes. . . .

[*He moves to the mirror, pacing about.*]

Yes. . . . Please. . . .

[*WOMAN picks up the magazine and
starts flipping through the pages. Pause.*]

Right. . . . No, no. . . . I will
call you back.
          –*Allez. Ciao.*

WOMAN: Who was it?

MAN: –A colleague.

WOMAN: I see.

[*Still looking at the magazine.*]

You walk about in circles lost inside

your score, with your
                 feet you draw
patterns on the wooden floor. . . .
You want me.
           You don't
want me. You must decide.

[*She puts the magazine down.*]

MAN: There is nothing to decide. These
are not the steps
             of the Viceregal Palace.
I do not stride up and down them
half naked with
            my sedition. –I have
always wanted you.
              I want you still.
I simply cannot suffer the consequences.

WOMAN: Tell me this is not the end.
It could not.
          I had been afraid.
Then the presentiment of things
turned real,
         the specter at last
become matter. Perhaps I shall
not be delivered
           from this.

[*She pours herself another drink.*]

MAN: I cannot say this way or that.
I have awakened
            to realize my

ultimate failure. A darkness injected
into my lifeline.
                    To realize this has
come back to me like an illness,
this unhappiness
                    like a boulder.
[*Pause.*]

I have loitered in old book stores
feeding a kind
                    of nostalgia.
I have sat in restaurants at closing,
watching the
                    orchestration of
the wait staff, wondering about
the empty lives
                    of others around me.
I have wandered through
blind alleyways
                    picking up
lost objects searching for a clue,
the mysterious
                    and insignificant
origin of things. I have not slept
in three days.
                    Tremors. Feverishness.
I fear I shall not last. My body
persists in a constant
                    state of shock.

[*He rubs his face.*]

Palpitations. Nervousness.
Anything I engage

                      seems not
without some major disturbance.

WOMAN: Was it any different before?

MAN: It used to be an affectation. Now
it is for real.

[*He paces to the window.*]

Art, poetry, philosophy. . . . What are
these things on a
                      cold winter night?
Rather, a glass of wine, a cigarette,
conversations at
                     a café, watching
the snow falling outside
in the muffled
                  streets. Wisdom
and knowledge. The enlightened
life and the
             life enjoyed.
Like music. Like a deadly sound.

[*He walks over to the mirror.*]

With this regression into that state,
unknown and
                at the same time
quite comforting, I have become
a strange sort
            of creature.

WOMAN: Beyond the surface motions of

a man deemed lost,
                  you seem quite
accustomed to your surroundings.
Your conspicuously
                  consumptive
musings have seized the greater part
of you, not allowing
                  for much else.

MAN: It seems I know nothing more.

WOMAN: This end, it had been pending
for some time.
                I no longer
inspire you. Perhaps I never did.

MAN: Forgone, I am not to be inspired.
I am like a wounded
                animal wandering
through the forest searching
for a ground.
              My life's endeavor,
thwarted, my requiem, unfound.

WOMAN: Always the martyr. Shame, you play
the part of saving
              me from yourself.
Why must the fidelity towards your ideas
presuppose a betrayal
              in your actions?

MAN: My life, my art. . . . If I stop, it stops.
I have come close
              to stopping.

WOMAN: Why would you do that? I had
believed we had
been committed
to this. Are we not sworn?

MAN: That is the sacrifice. Disavow
this union.
Too late now to be
contesting that turn, the reduction
of that constancy
inherent in design.
Dignified, you persist in invoking
this commitment
and proclaiming
everything by it. We would have
done better to
elevate ourselves
to be worthy of this bond we had
consecrated.
This is where
we find ourselves, surrounded by
the furnishings of
a disappointed life.
It was our undoing and we shall
be undone again.
We suffer the opiates
and safeguard our denial. We watch
the candles lit
in vigil slowly burn.
We will not alter their course.

WOMAN: Please. You will make me cry.

MAN: I have made you cry too often.

[*MAN and WOMAN rotate so WOMAN is
backstage, MAN in front, facing each other.*]

I have realized once again what I have
known. The grand
      overture sustains.

WOMAN: You speak of sacrifice, but what
     could you possibly
          know if it
     with your twice faltered rebirth?

MAN: In order to possess you I must
    let you go, it is
         said. In order
    to find you, I must leave.

WOMAN: –Enough. Go then, if you must.

     [*Pause. WOMAN looking away.*]

MAN: If I leave now, it will be the end.

    [*Pause. MAN grasping at his throat.*]

WOMAN: So be it. There can be nothing
     more. There is no
          looking back.
     You know the drill.

MAN: As you wish.

    [*Lights dim.*]

SCENE V

[*MAN stands in the back, WOMAN in
the front, both facing outward. Camera
equipment is packed away. As they speak,
they slowly pace around the chairs so
MAN will end front stage.*]

WOMAN: You have prepared your things.

MAN: I should be leaving.

[*Pause.*]

Will I see you again?

WOMAN: Perhaps, yes. No. I do not know.
What would you
        have me say?

MAN: Because we have hurt each other
and because
        we continue
to hurt each other. Because
you have
        implored me to stop
the suffering and to take back
the vows. Because
        I have fallen from
your grace. Because I have regressed
into that state
        of desiring nothing.
I have become lost. I have

rendered myself
          to that oblivion
of sleep that I might become
one with the
          void around me.
A slow seduction into darker waters,
black pools of
          constant calling,
lapping without a glimmer.
Knowing now
          what it is to be
damaged. To have found love,
but then to
          realize I was not
meant for it. To be near the thing
that mattered, then
          to be made distant.

WOMAN: The widening waters erase
both memory
          and want.
This drink I have been treated,
I press my fingers
          against it and
bring it to my lips. To tender all hope
for a moment regained.
          Original. Pure.
To cause a thing of infinite effect.
No longer a matter
          of good or right,
to return to the site of the first
undoing, the last
          movement of
defiance. Until my weeping

becomes punctual
        and thereby
absent of meaning. And all my sorrows
become a thing
        of useless beauty.

MAN: To be transformed into someone
whole and complete
        for a time,
then to be that man no longer.
To go on, to be
        unfound and to be
erased of all sounds.

WOMAN: My efforts deflected by your strict stance.
Having seen this
        thing and that thing
crossing one empty place to the next,
you, architect of time,
        collapsing space.
I shudder. And I have no influence.

MAN: Without possession, only memories
now remain,
        your constant
search in the dark for my hand
in your sleep,
        and mornings when
I opened my eyes to see you
refreshed, your
        peignoir which
seemed to always sense my desire,
or when you would
        blow into my ears,

or play with my hair and I acted annoyed,
all your mispronounced
                                  words you read
somewhere but never heard spoken. . . .
And your half steps
                                  in the cold,
bundled up so only your eyes
had shown, the way
                                  you could hear
the same passage of a song, over
and again and still
                                  marvel at the same
moments, your delight which could not
be defeated, but
                                  I have defeated.

WOMAN: So I carry on, tentative and
uncontested,
                                  attentive only
to the present. Your words and
gestures of
                                  nothing at all,
returned to their place of cruelty
and rhetoric.
                                  And I, thinking,
if it happens that we see each other
again, will we
                                  recognize it?
With a practiced tongue to end
with one last
                                  impertinent word,
a sigh, a turn. A single act.

MAN: –Please forgive me. All this endless

beauty taken
for granted, now
an empty crater in my heart
I must bear.
I shall remember
these things, things which would
fulfill a life for a man
who is not forgone.
All but to remember that we had
loved much, though
perhaps not well.

WOMAN: Waiting for the day where some
instance of certain
wonderment
might show itself with belated bliss.
No longer with
any claim
in the real, my past disintegrated
into shards of
reticence and regret.
While I wait the night with infusions
of wine and
stars and tears,
until each trepidatious flame
is then finally
extinguished.

MAN: And if it were to be that somehow
we could live on
without regret,
and that you might hold dear
those few moments
when we were

happy, that would be enough
to preserve me.

WOMAN: My longings, cast like a boat adrift
on the headless
                waves, its flags
windless and without a calling.
To be transformed
                again, as, after
a sudden downpour, the moment
when the rain
            is missed.
Some essence perhaps achieved
but not to be
              transmitted, like
last season's leaves amidst the dead.

MAN: And so it goes, to continue
on this course,
             taking my coffee
and cigarettes, moving from place
to place, headless
            as before.

[*He picks up a photo, looks at it.*]

I shall survive this strain
all the days of
           my life. And
from time to time, I shall look
upon your image
           and think
of the happiness I had–something
of which in my
           essence I was

not deserving. And I shall weep
in utter sorrow
                for this day, knowing
in my deepest core my desire
for you remains,
                despite everything,
but also knowing that I could not
make you happy
                in this world, this life.
All but to remember that I loved you.
And to continue
                to love you.
For we shall reunite again, in another
world, another life.
                –Goodbye.

[*MAN begins to walk forward. He pauses
near the edge of the stage. He looks
at the photo, then looks outward.*]

WOMAN: This final assimilation of sleep
        descends upon me,
                slowly expanding
        white as death from contingent forms
        stitched, winged
                silhouettes torn
        from flight. Ascension foiled.
        Bewitched dreams
                awakened to
        the travesty of day. Unsettled
        like a star. Appended
                to no avail,
        this passionless procession of maidens,
        endless without
                any beginning.

A sacrifice without signs. Once
so elate. Replete.
                    Completely alive.
Now dislocated. To be left alone
to navigate this
                    world, this life
without charm.

[MAN, *without moving his body, slowly*
turns his head towards WOMAN.]

                    –My angel
defeated. My deliverance void.

[*Lights out on WOMAN, lights out on MAN.*]

[*CURTAIN.*]

BY THE AUTHOR

Epitaph
(Forthcoming)

Exit Orpheus
2009

I, Faust
2007

Cities & Dust
(Abstracts published as the Appendix to *I, Faust*)